In the Doctors' Surgery

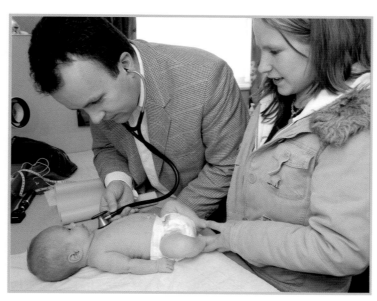

Ruth Thomson

WAYLAND

First published in 2006 by Wayland,
an imprint of Hachette Children's Books

Editor: Laura Milne
Managing Editor: Victoria Brooker
Senior Design Manager: Rosamund Saunders

Design: Proof Books
Commissioned photography: Chris Fairclough

British Library Cataloguing in Publication Data:

Thomson, Ruth
Helping hands in the doctors' surgery
1. Medical centres – Juvenile literature
2. Medical personnel – Juvenile literature
I. Title II. In the doctors' surgery
362.1'2

ISBN-10: 0-7502-4854-8
ISBN-13: 978-0-7502-4854-9

Printed and bound in China

Hachette Children's Books
A division of Hodder Headline Limited
338 Euston Road, London NW1 3BH

Acknowledgements
The author and publisher would like to thank the following
people for their help and participation in this book: Heather
Heatley, Wendy Fernie, Dr Jonathan Heatley, Dr Chris Heath,
Dr Hwa-Lon Liu, Dr Ajaz Sheikh, Dr Paul Woods, Dr Nadia
Ziyada, Carol Lewis, Kay Barrington, Beatrice Maddison,
Sabrina Gant, Emma Gant, Sonal Patel, Omid Chiang, Linda
Mole, Tim Jolly, Zarina Bangie, Amy Bangie, Karen Killerby,
Christine Halliday, Joe Wells, Alison Woods, Kirsty Woods,
Evie Woods, J Sledmar, Abbie Sledmar, Amelia Ng, Nick
Heatley, Czeslaw Soltysik, Mary Pascoe, Amanda Barnett,
Trinia Lewis, Charlie Wingfield, Helen Power and Cecilia Terry
at Holbrook Surgery, Horsham.

'5 A Day – Just Eat More (Fruit and Veg)', published by the
Department of Health, Crown Copyright, 2003.
'FACT – Secondhand smoke is a killer', published by the
Department of Health, Crown Copyright'
'How safe is your child from burns and scalds',
© Child Accident Prevention Trust 2002.

Contents

Words printed in **bold** are explained in the glossary.

The team

We work at a doctors' **surgery**. The doctors and nurses see **patients** who are ill or hurt or who need a check-up or **immunisations**. The office staff help organise the surgery and make sure it runs well.

▲ We are the doctors.   ▲ We are the nurses.

The surgery is built on two floors. The **reception**, waiting area and doctors' rooms are on the ground floor.

▲ The office staff work upstairs.

▲ We are the office staff.

Receptionists

We are receptionists. We take it in turns to do all sorts of different jobs.

▼ We open letters and put them into pigeon-holes for each doctor.

▲ We answer the phones and make **appointments** for **patients**.

Some patients arrive for an appointment. Others come to collect **prescriptions**.

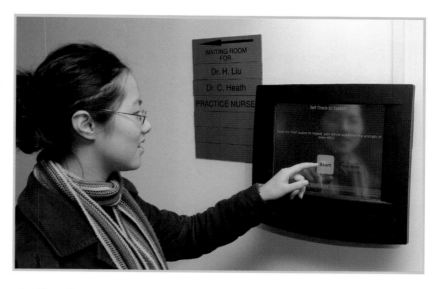

▲ Patients can check in for their appointment on a computer screen.

▼ We greet patients at the reception desk.

The practice manager

I work in the office at the doctors' surgery. I make sure the surgery runs well, and I make plans for its future.

▼ I keep our medical records up-to-date.

▲ I discuss ways to give patients the best care.

Once a week, all the doctors and nurses
have lunch together in our meeting room.

▲ Sometimes I arrange for speakers
to come and talk at our lunches.

The doctors

The doctors see patients at the **surgery** twice a day, once in the morning and once in the afternoon.

People sit in the waiting area for their turn to see a doctor. ▶

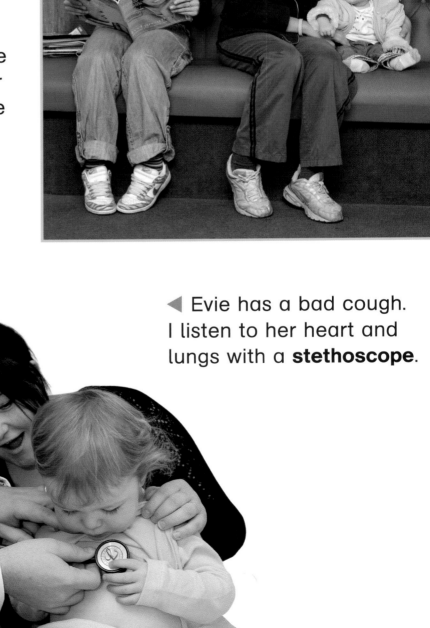

◀ Evie has a bad cough. I listen to her heart and lungs with a **stethoscope**.

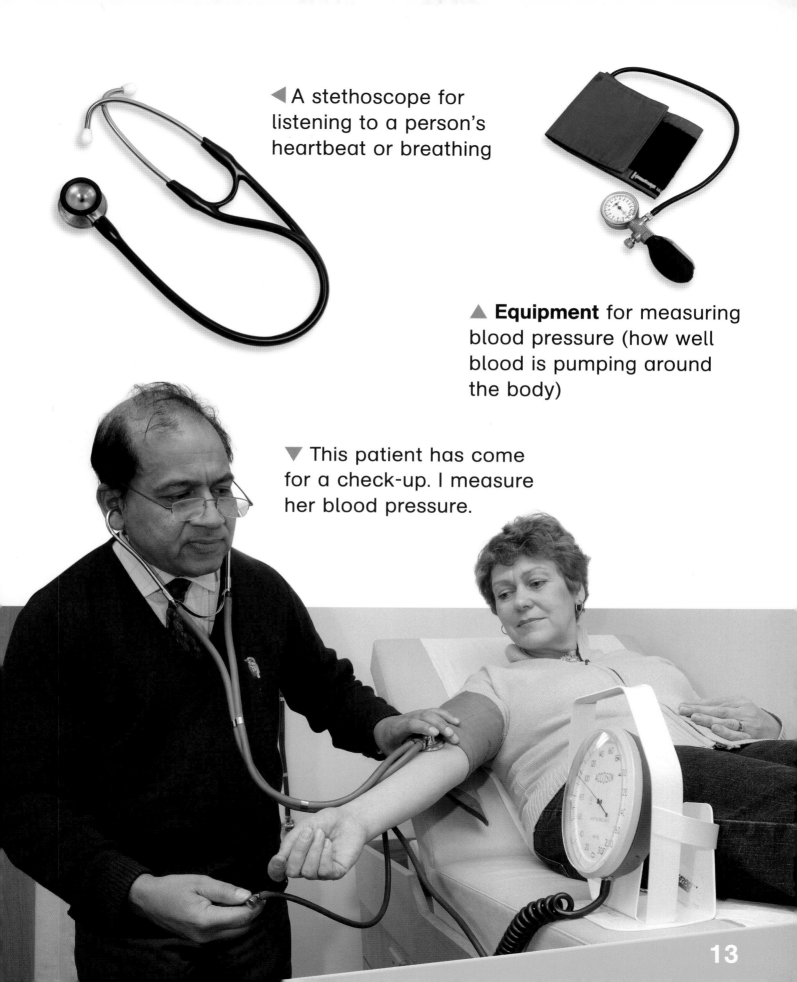

◀ A stethoscope for listening to a person's heartbeat or breathing

▲ **Equipment** for measuring blood pressure (how well blood is pumping around the body)

▼ This patient has come for a check-up. I measure her blood pressure.

Doctors' work

We are busy
all day long.

I do minor **operations**.
Here I am taking out
some **stitches.**
A nurse helps me. ▶

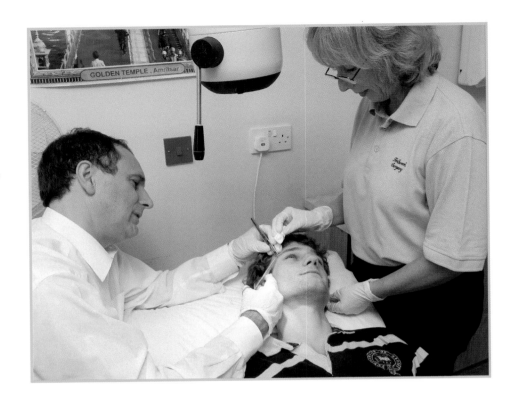

◀ I write out
prescriptions for
medicines.

We use all sorts of **equipment** at the surgery.

A **thermometer**

A hammer for testing **reflexes**

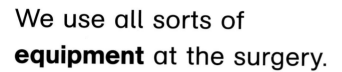
Crocodile forceps for holding skin firmly in place

Syringes for **injections**

Syringe needles

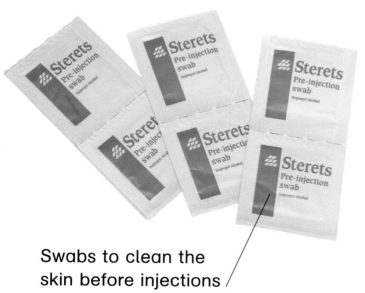
Swabs to clean the skin before injections

Spatulas for holding down the tongue

15

Special interests

Each doctor also has a special interest in certain parts of the body.

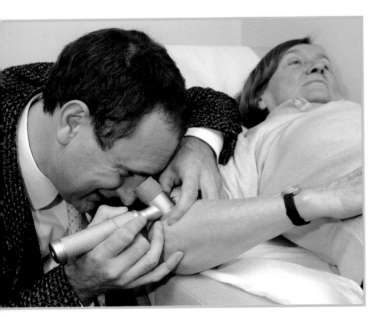

▲ I help people who have rashes or sore and itchy skin.

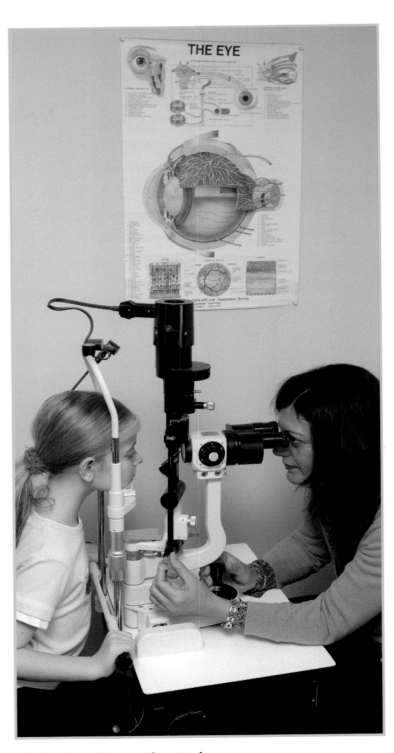

THE EYE

▲ I check **patients'** eyes to see if they are healthy.

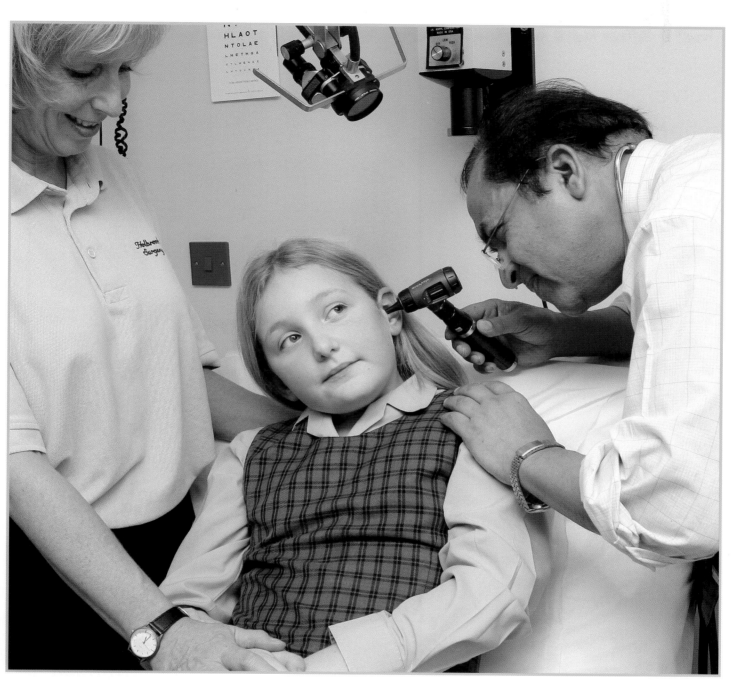

▲ I look after patients who have problems with their ears, noses or throats.

◀ I use an auroscope to see inside the ear.

Check-ups for babies

I give babies a check-up when they are six weeks old, to make sure they are growing properly.

I listen to Charlie's heart and lungs with a **stethoscope.** ▶

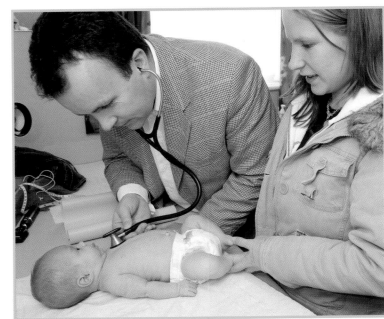

I check he can hold up his head. ▶

I hold up a fluffy ball and see if Charlie follows it with his eyes. ▶

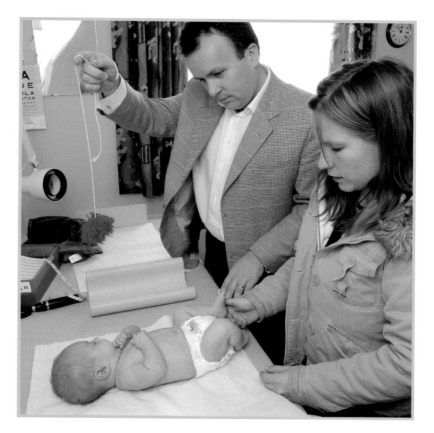

▼ The nurse gives Charlie **immunisations** against childhood diseases.

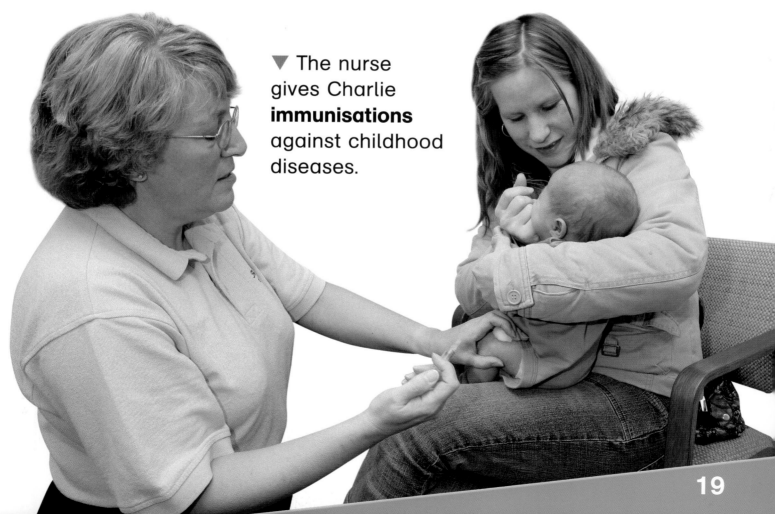

Practice nurses

We are practice nurses. We have a room of our own. People make **appointments** to see us. We also help the doctors.

▼ I give **injections** to people who are travelling abroad.

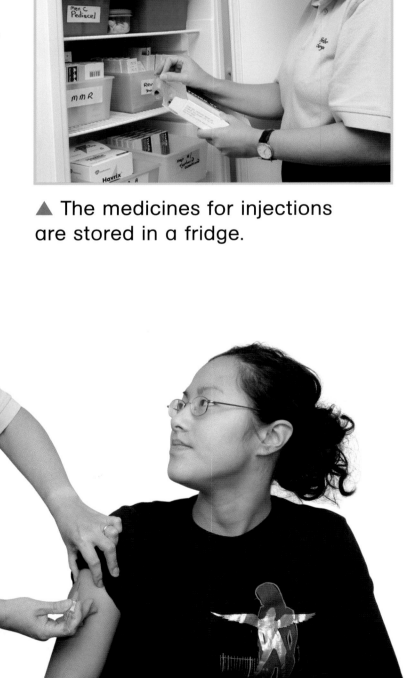

▲ The medicines for injections are stored in a fridge.

We look after patients with **asthma**. We show patients how to use an inhaler to help with their breathing.

▲ Inhalers

▼ We test how well a patient breathes.

Help and advice

As well as helping ill people, we give advice to people on how they can stay healthy and fit. We talk to them about food, exercise, sleep and smoking.

▲ I explain to this patient how to sit so that he does not strain his back.

Big models of cigarettes hang in the waiting room to warn people about the dangers of smoking. ▼

▲ There are all sorts of useful leaflets in the waiting room that people can read.

◄ I am a physiotherapist. I treat people with back and neck pain or sprains. I give people exercises to do.

Healthy eating

* Eat plenty of fruit and vegetables.

* Eat starchy foods, such as bread, potatoes, noodles, pasta and rice, to give you energy.

* Drink milk and eat yogurt and cheese to keep your bones and teeth strong.

* Eat foods such as meat, fish, eggs, beans and nuts, to help your body grow and repair itself.

The health visitor

I visit newborn babies at home, to check that they are feeding well and putting on weight.

I also run a baby clinic at the **surgery**.

▲ Emma is 8 months old. I show her a book to see how alert she is.

I give Emma some building bricks to see how good she is with her hands. ▼

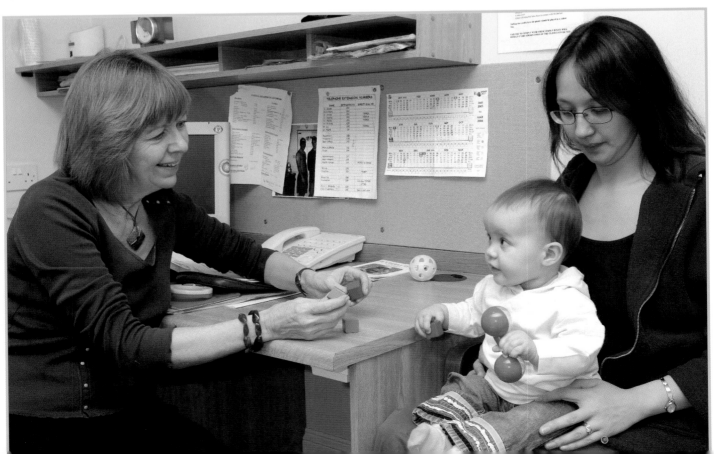

It is important to check how well young children are growing.

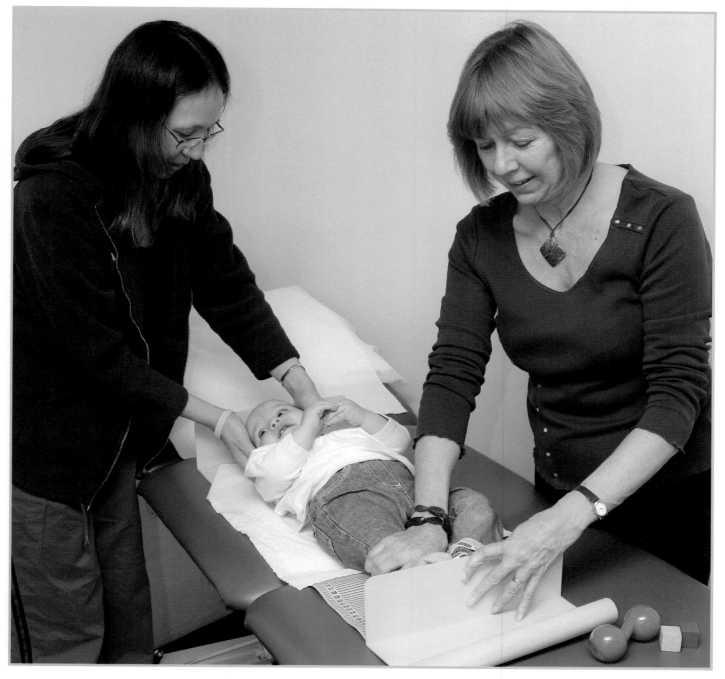

▲ I measure how long Emma is.

District nurses

We visit patients who are too ill
or too old to come to the doctors'
surgery. We see them in their own homes.

I take all
the **equipment**
I need in
a bag. ▶

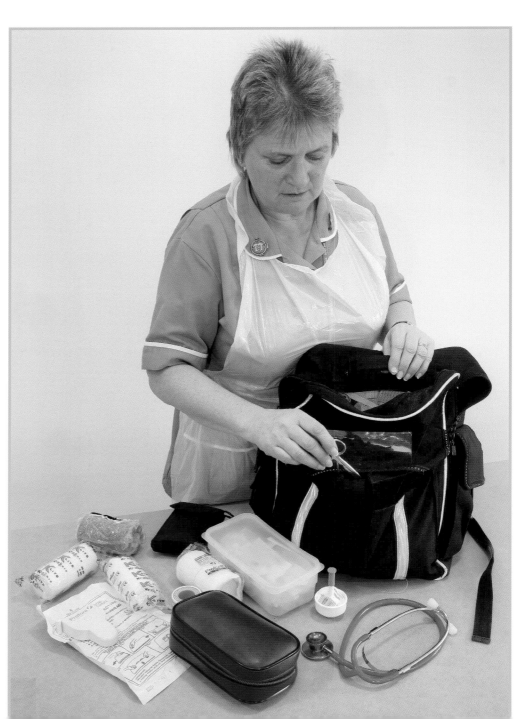

▲ Today, I have come to change Beatrice's **dressing**.

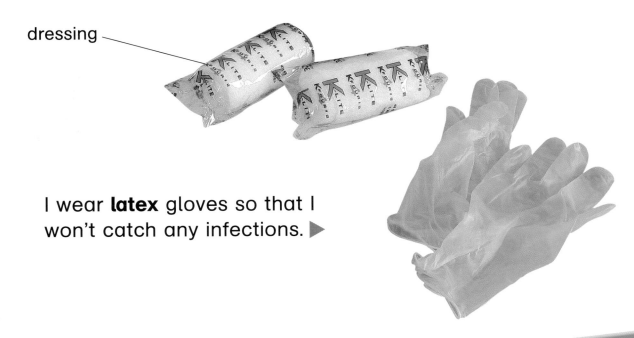

dressing

I wear **latex** gloves so that I won't catch any infections. ▶

Glossary

appointment a time when a doctor or nurse agrees to see a patient

asthma an illness that makes breathing difficult

dressing a covering, such as a bandage or plaster, for a cut or burn

equipment all the things that people use for their job

injection putting something into a person's body using a syringe and needle

immunisation putting a substance into a person's body to stop them getting an illness

latex thin, stretchy rubber

operation something done by a doctor to remove part of a person's body or to treat a disease

patient a person who is looked after by a doctor or nurse

prescription a doctor's written note that says what medicine a patient needs

reception the place where patients check in for their appointment

reflexes automatic movements that a person can't control. Doctors tap a patient's knee with a hammer to check their reflexes.

stethoscope an instrument doctors use to listen to a person's heart and lungs

stitches loops made with special thread to keep the edges of a cut together

surgery the place where doctors or dentists examine patients

syringe a small cylinder with a needle attached. It is used for taking blood out of a person's body or for injections.

thermometer an instrument that measures how hot or cold someone is

Quiz

Look back through the book to do this quiz.

1 Who works at a doctor's surgery?
2 What happens at a baby's check-up?
3 What do physiotherapists do?
4 What is a prescription?
5 Who does a health visitor look after?
6 How do nurses help people with asthma?
7 Who does a district nurse look after?

Answers

1 Doctors, nurses and office staff
2 A doctor checks that the baby is growing properly.
3 They treat back and neck pain, sprains and sore muscles.
4 A doctor's written note that says what medicine a patient needs
5 Babies and young children
6 They test breathing and show patients how to use an inhaler.
7 People who are too ill or too old to visit the surgery

Useful contacts

www.cpsc.gov/kids/kidssafety
An American website with quizzes about how to avoid accidents on a bike, skateboarding, in the playground or at home.

www.welltown.gov.uk
A website for 5-7 year olds with tips and games about keeping safe and healthy at home, in the playground, in the sun and at school.

It is the people who make the job. We have a fantastic team spirit and always support one another.

Index